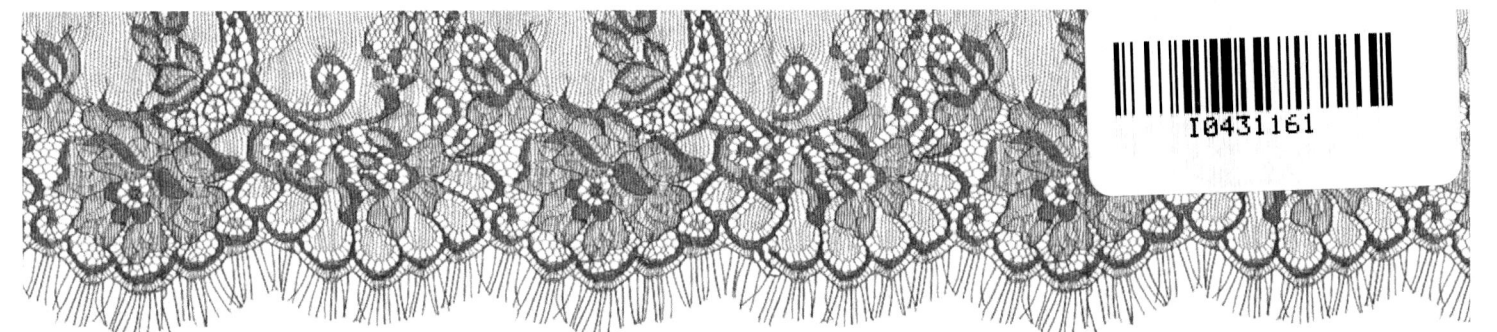

Snowflake Art: Christmas Spirit

Level 2: Intermediate

Written and Designed by
Erica Alldredge of the Papercut Prodigy Team

Dedicated to my mother and father,
who always encouraged my artistic side.

Warning:
These snowflakes are not for the faint of heart!
Each one is more difficult than the last.
Do you dare take the challenge?

Copyright Erica Bates Alldredge 2022 © Papercut Prodigy Team
For more of my artwork visit my Etsy Shop:
Papercut Prodigy: https://www.etsy.com/shop/PapercutProdigy

Table of Contents

	Tips for Cutting	1
	How to Fold 4 and 6 Pointed Snowflakes	2
	Preserving and Displaying Your Snowflakes	3
Very Easy	Candy Canes	4
	Poinsettia	5
	Gingerbread Man	6
Easy	Stocking	7
	Ornaments	8
Moderate	Presents under the Tree	9
	Star of Bethlehem	10
	Saint Lucia	11
	Jacks	12
	Santa	13
Getting Harder	Snowman	14
	Pinebough	15
	Snowglobe	16
Very Hard	Shepherds	17
	Holly Wreath	18
	Jingle Bells	19
Holy Smokes!	Reindeer	20
	Elves	21
	Light Tangle	22
	Nutcracker Suite	23

Tips for Cutting:

- Every design in this book can be cut out with scissors - a detail knife is not necessary, but can be used if you prefer. It's a good idea to use either a familiar pair of very sharp scissors, or an Exacto knife with a new blade. Be very careful and don't cut anything but paper!

- If you do use a detail blade, make sure you have a mat or piece of cardboard under the design so you don't cut your table.

- Paper has a thickness, so each section will be slightly different. If you fold the paper carefully and crease it as you go, the difference will be less noticeable. Fold carefully!!

- 6 pointed snowflakes will always be harder to cut than 4 pointed ones because you're cutting through 4 more layers of paper. The design is also narrower.

- Be aware of the positive and negative shapes you're working with. The positive shapes are the white part of the design you'll be leaving. The negative shapes are the shaded areas you'll be cutting away. Both parts are equally important to the design of the snowflake.

- The biggest problem you'll have is slippage, which is when the lower folds slide away from the upper folds as you cut. This causes the design to be off, and if it's bad enough, you can accidentally cut through a positive design!

- The best trick to avoid slippage is to hold the paper tightly and carefully, and pay attention as you're cutting. Another thing you can do is cut a straight line down a negative space you're not going to cut out yet. Then push one side of the pattern up, and the other down. This will help you to align the paper again when you get to that spot, and stop it from slipping until then.

- Start cutting at the farthest tip from the center of the snowflake. This is where most slippage happens, so you can minimize that by starting from the outside and working toward the center. It's especially important for 4 pointed designs, which are more likely to slip.

- Most importantly, and this can't be emphasized enough - have fun! It can be intriguing to follow an intricate design and the challenge it presents. There is much satisfaction to be had in the completion of such a difficult project. We hope you enjoy these designs.

Preserving and Displaying Your Snowflakes:

- Be sure to cut out all of the negative design before unfolding your snowflake. Be very careful as you open it so it doesn't tear.

- If you're having trouble getting your snowflake to lay flat, you can carefully press it flat inside a large book for a few hours.

- The best way to preserve your snowflake is to laminate it. A personal laminator is best because you can lay the design out flat inside the sleeve before running it through the machine. You can also find a laminator at most print shops - some are even self-serve! Be very careful to lay your snowflake flat so it doesn't fold over itself as it is encased in plastic.

- Once it is laminated, carefully cut the plastic around the design, at least 1/4 inch away from the paper. You can chose to cut the plastic in a circle around the design, or undulate closer to the design itself. Then just tape your snowflake to a window or attach a string and hang it from the ceiling! These make beautiful decorations for any home or office.

- If you don't have access to a laminator, you can gently place the snowflake in a clear plastic sheet protector, which are available anywhere you can get stationary. Display it inside the protector.

- If you want to attach your snowflake to a dark poster board or backing, we recommend laying it out flat on newspaper and using spray fixative on the 'front' side of the snowflake (the side that was printed on.) Carefully stick it to the board so the 'back' side is displayed. Make sure you spray in a well ventilated area and hold the spray fixative at least 18 inches from the snowflake so that it doesn't get blown over by the force of the spray and get glue on both sides.

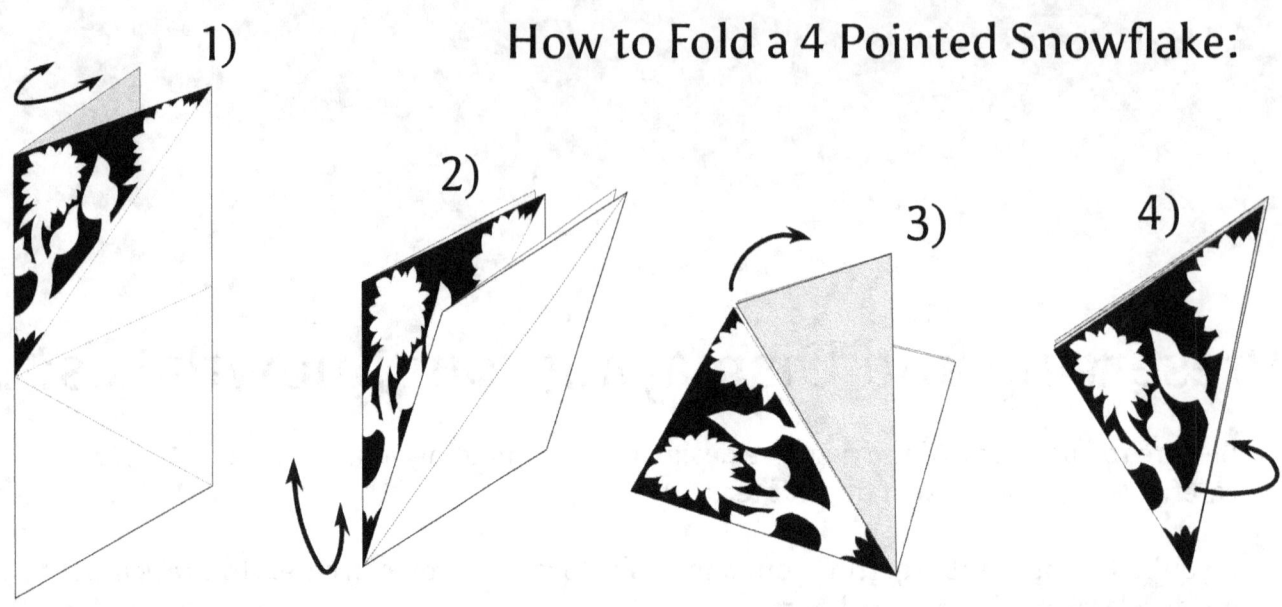

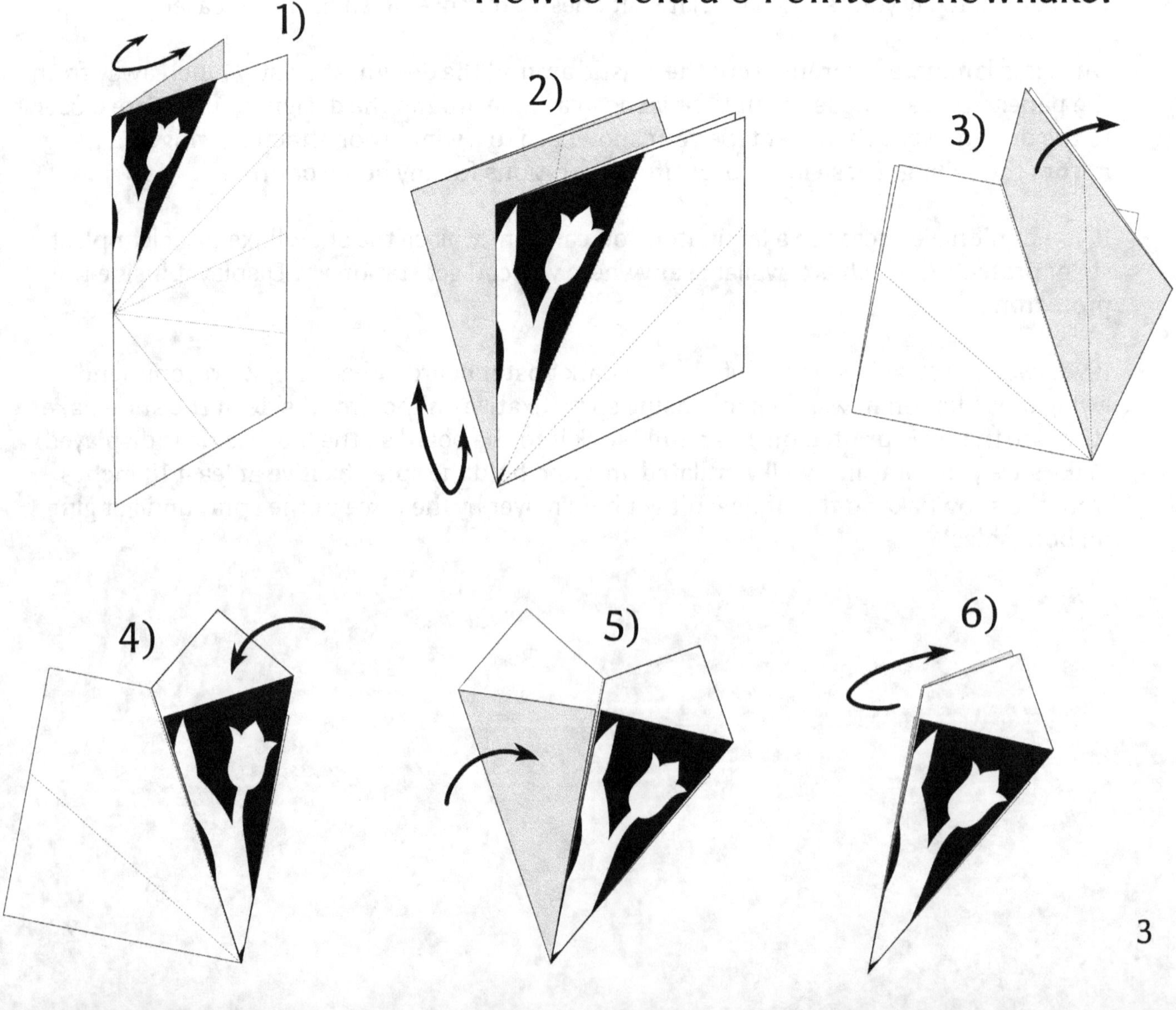

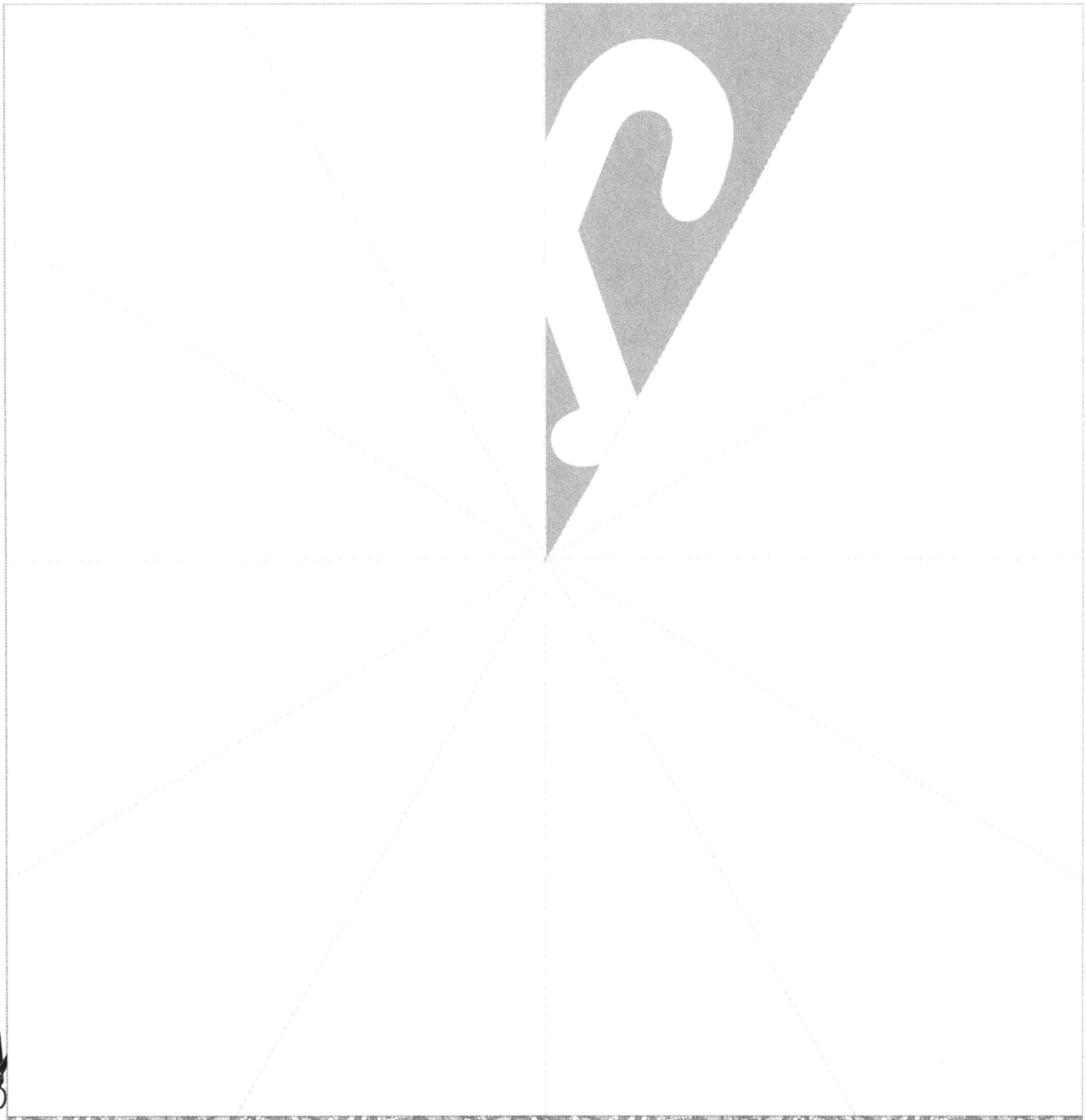

Candy Canes
6 Pointed, Very Easy

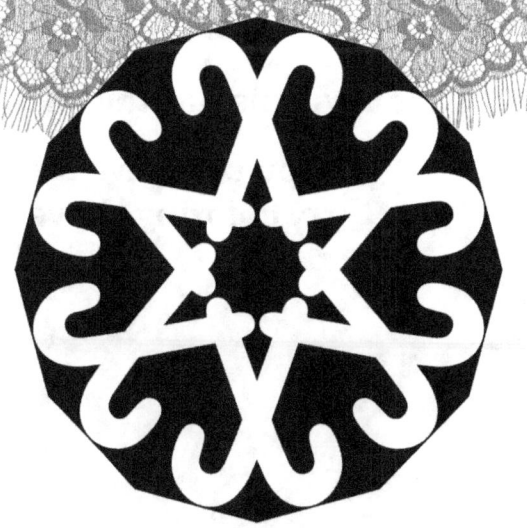

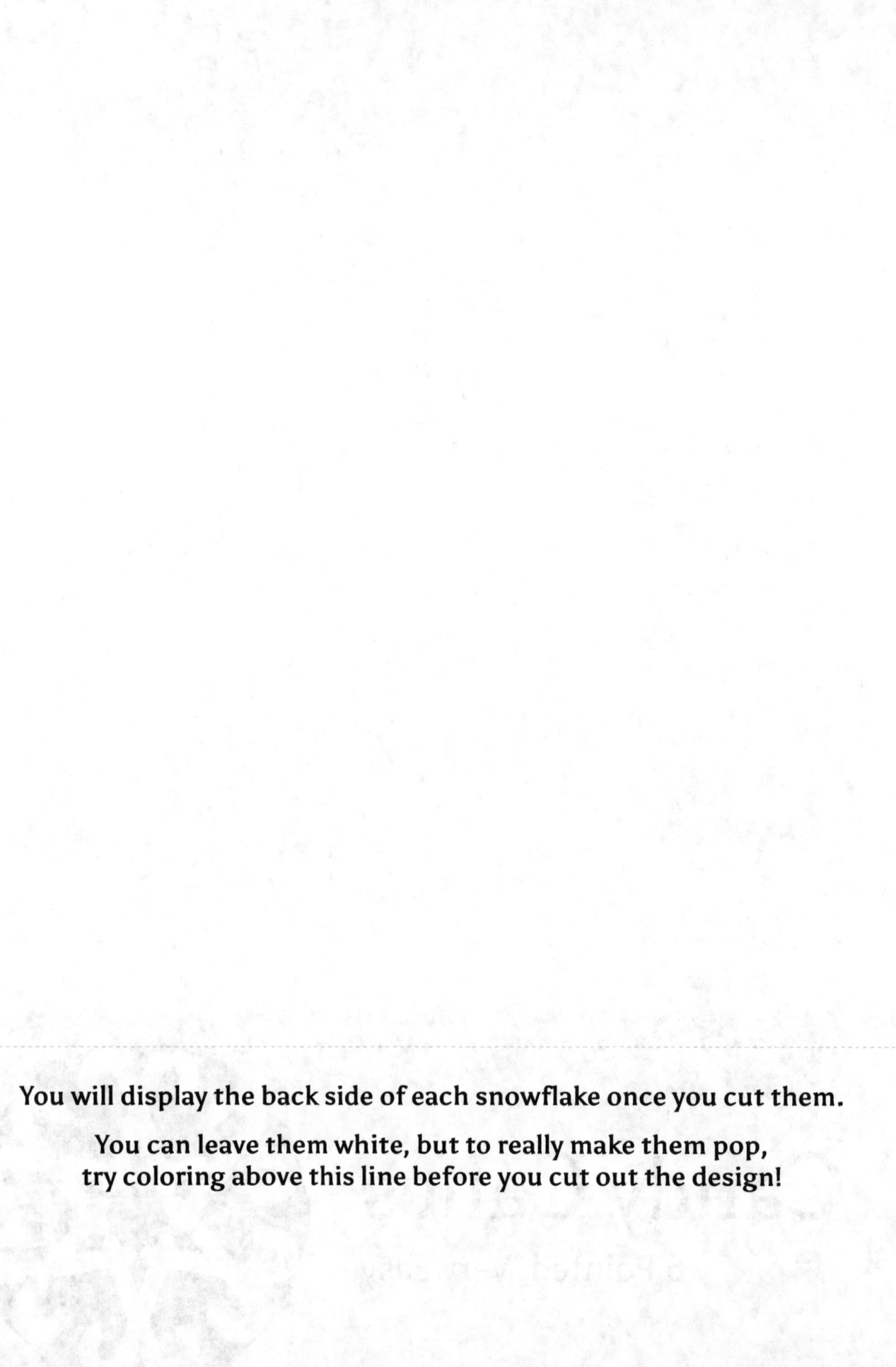

You will display the back side of each snowflake once you cut them.

You can leave them white, but to really make them pop,
try coloring above this line before you cut out the design!

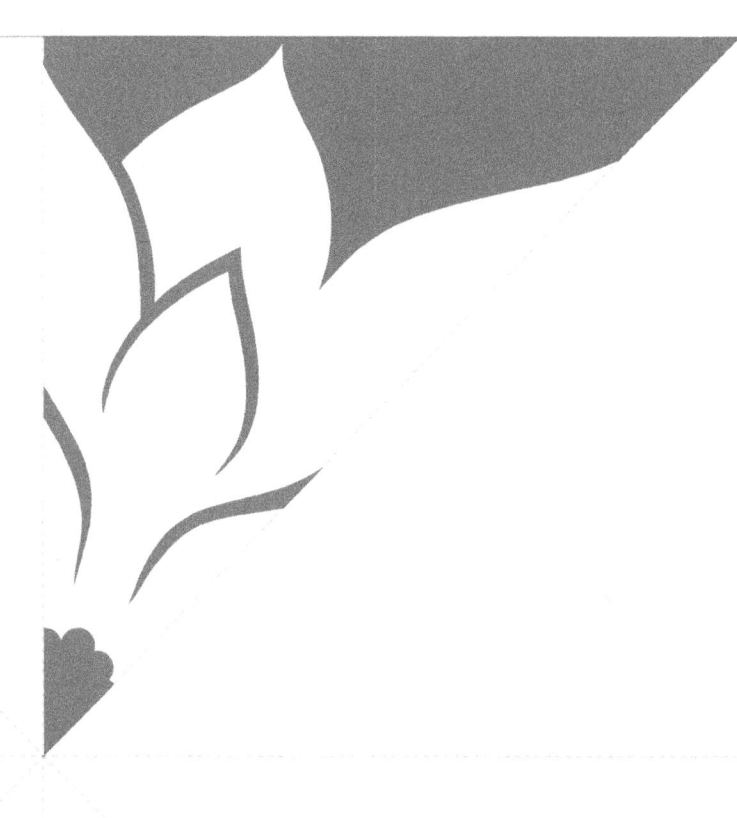

Poinsettia
4 Pointed, Very Easy

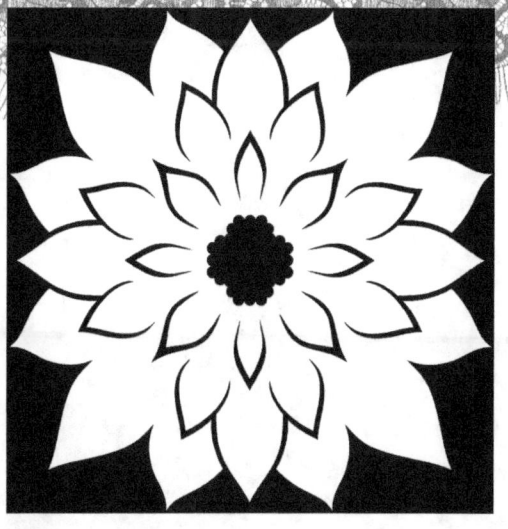

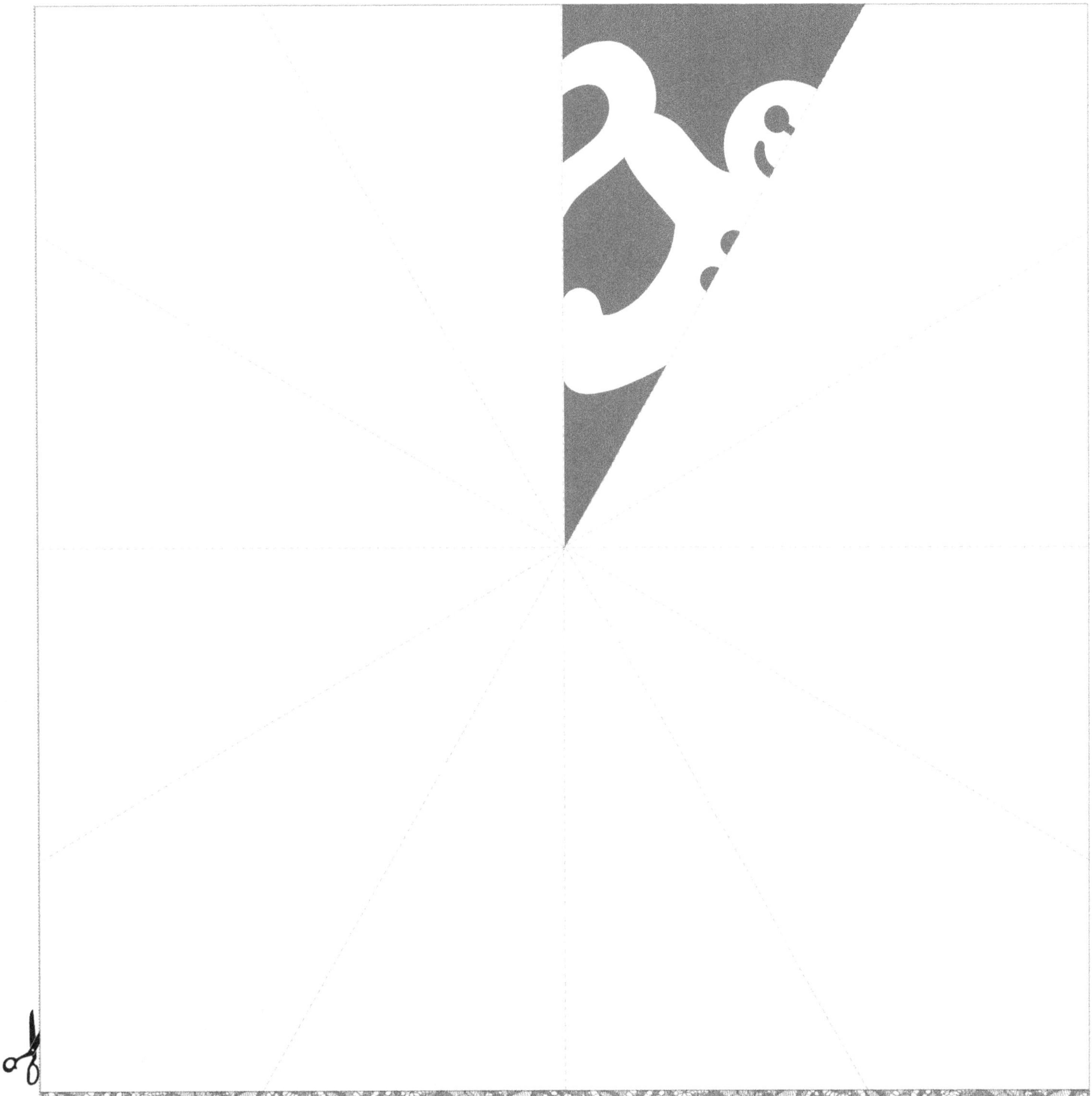

Gingerbread Man

6 Pointed, Very Easy

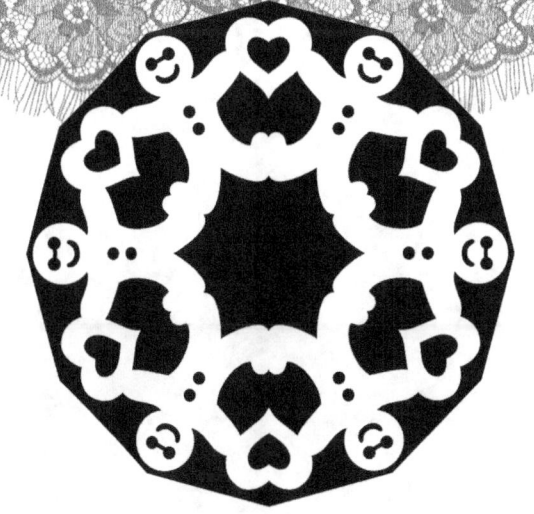

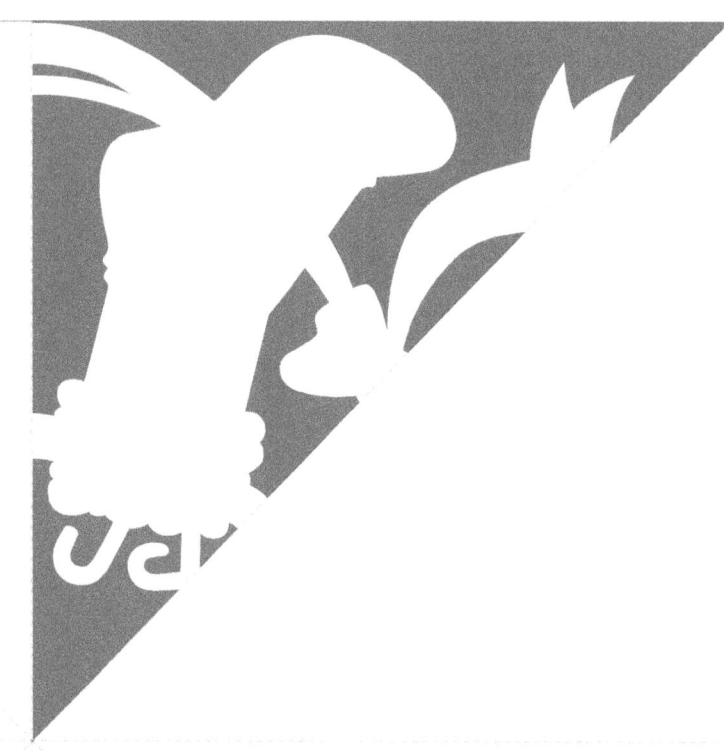

Stockings
4 Pointed, Easy

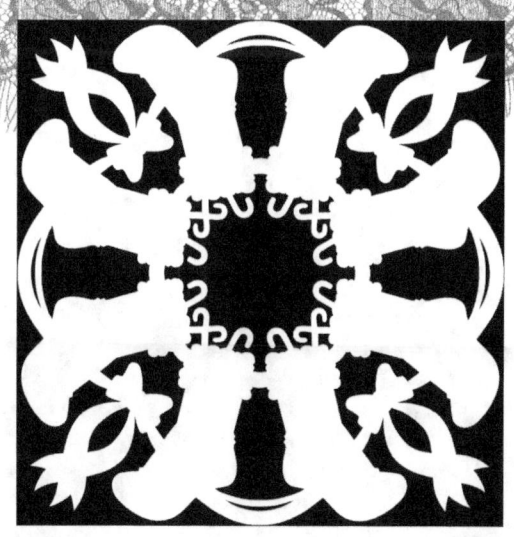

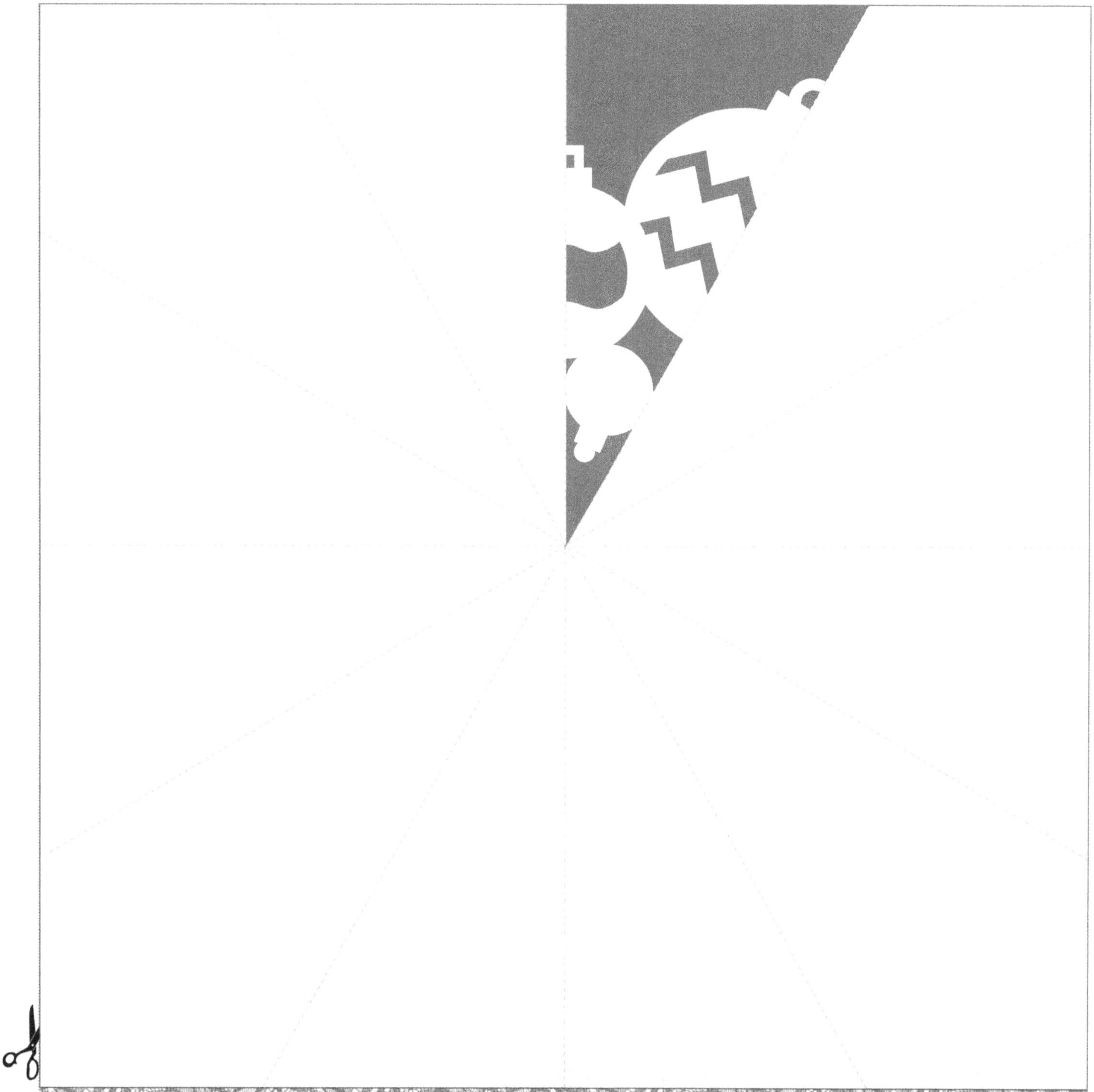

Ornaments

6 Pointed, Easy

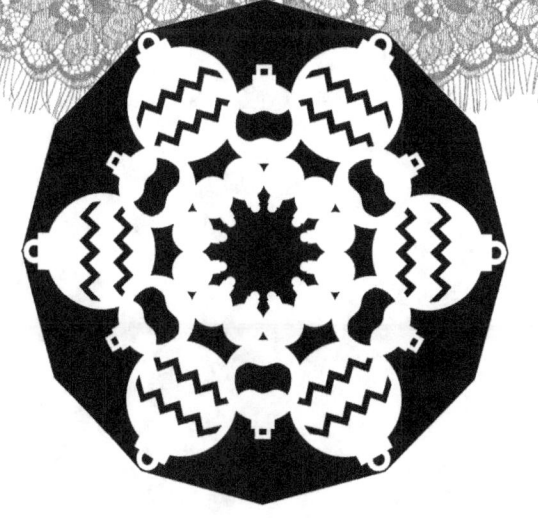

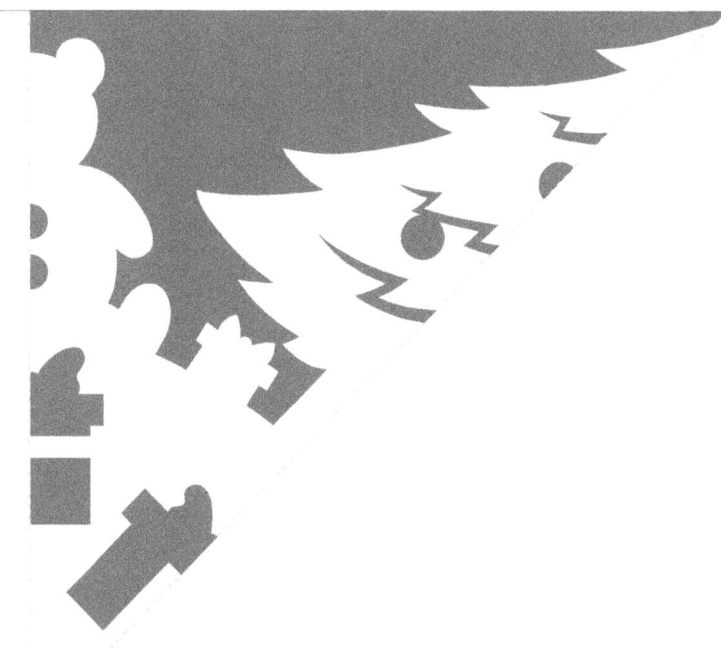

Presents under the Tree
4 Pointed, Moderate

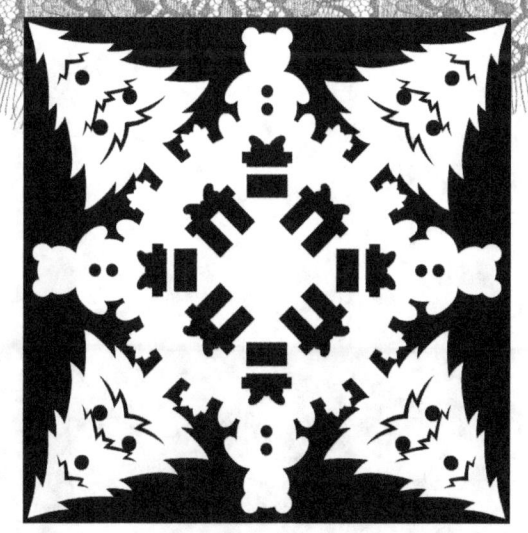

Star of Bethlehem

6 Pointed, Moderate

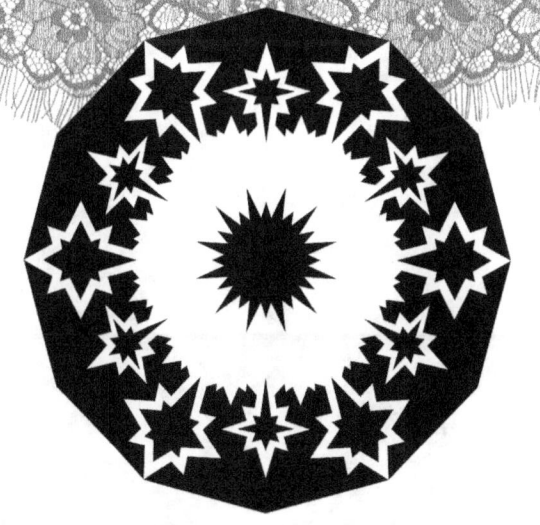

10

Saint Lucia
4 Pointed, Moderate

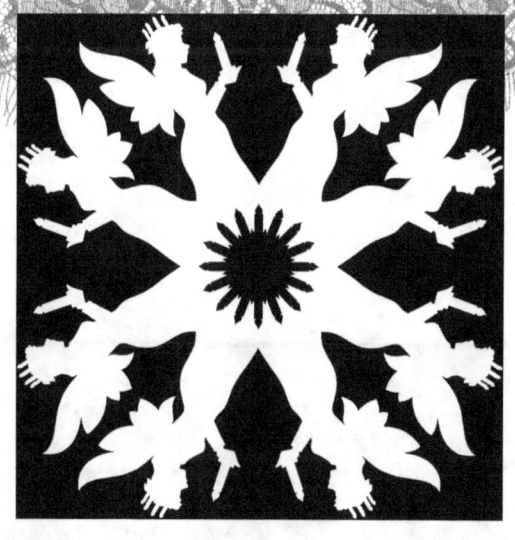

Jacks
6 Pointed, Moderate

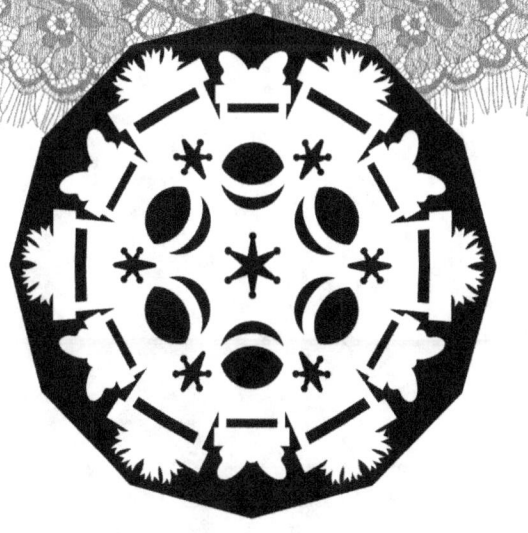

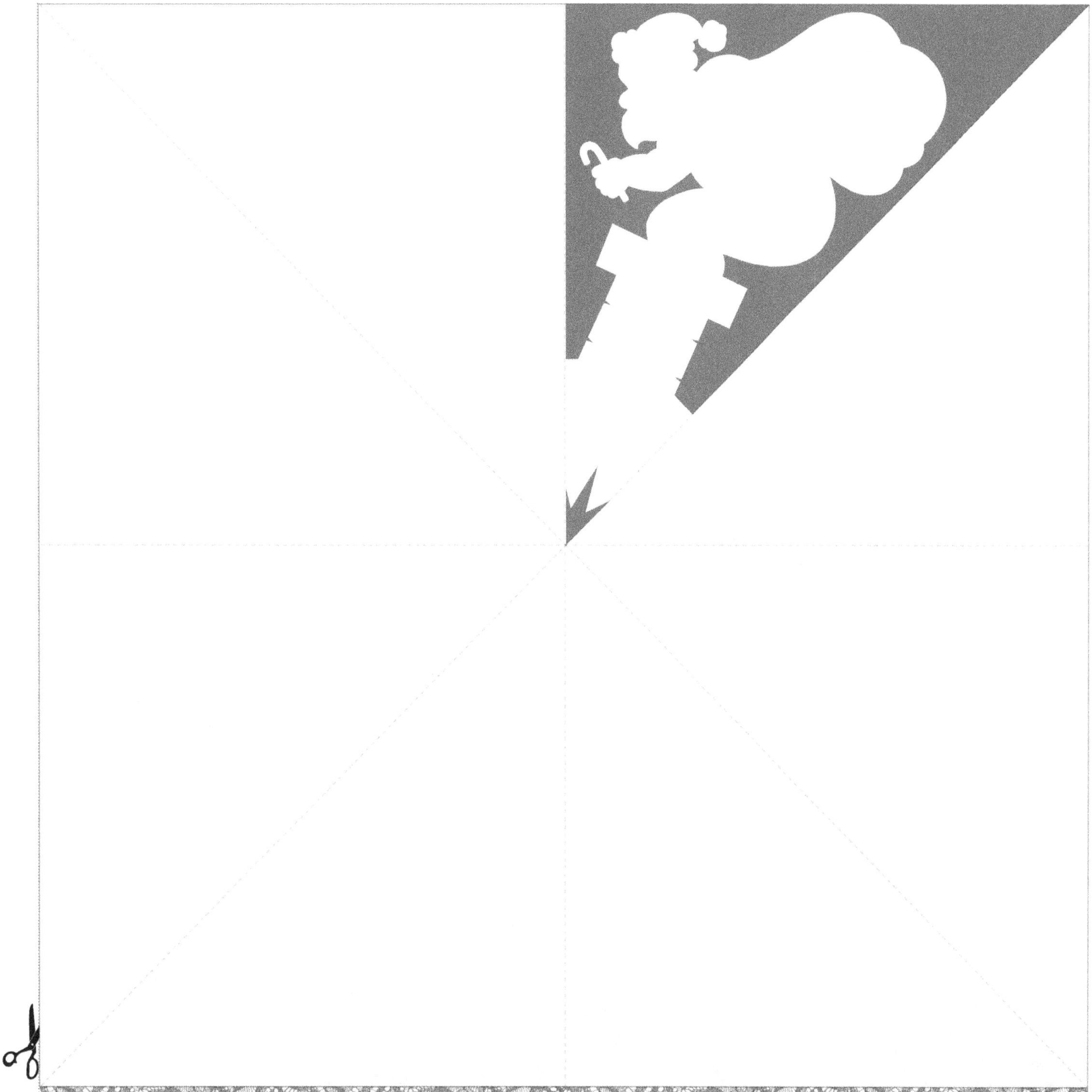

Santa
4 Pointed, Moderate

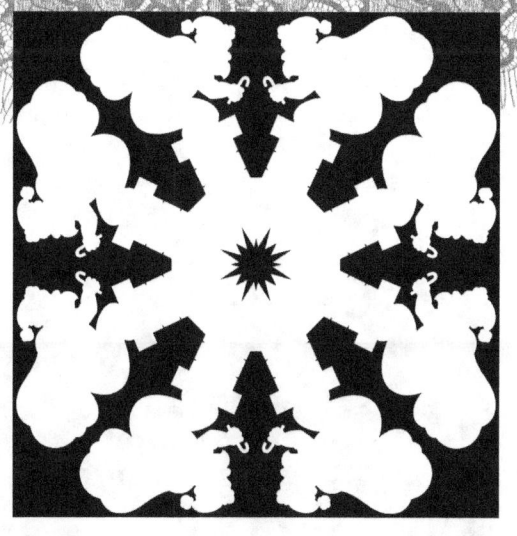

13

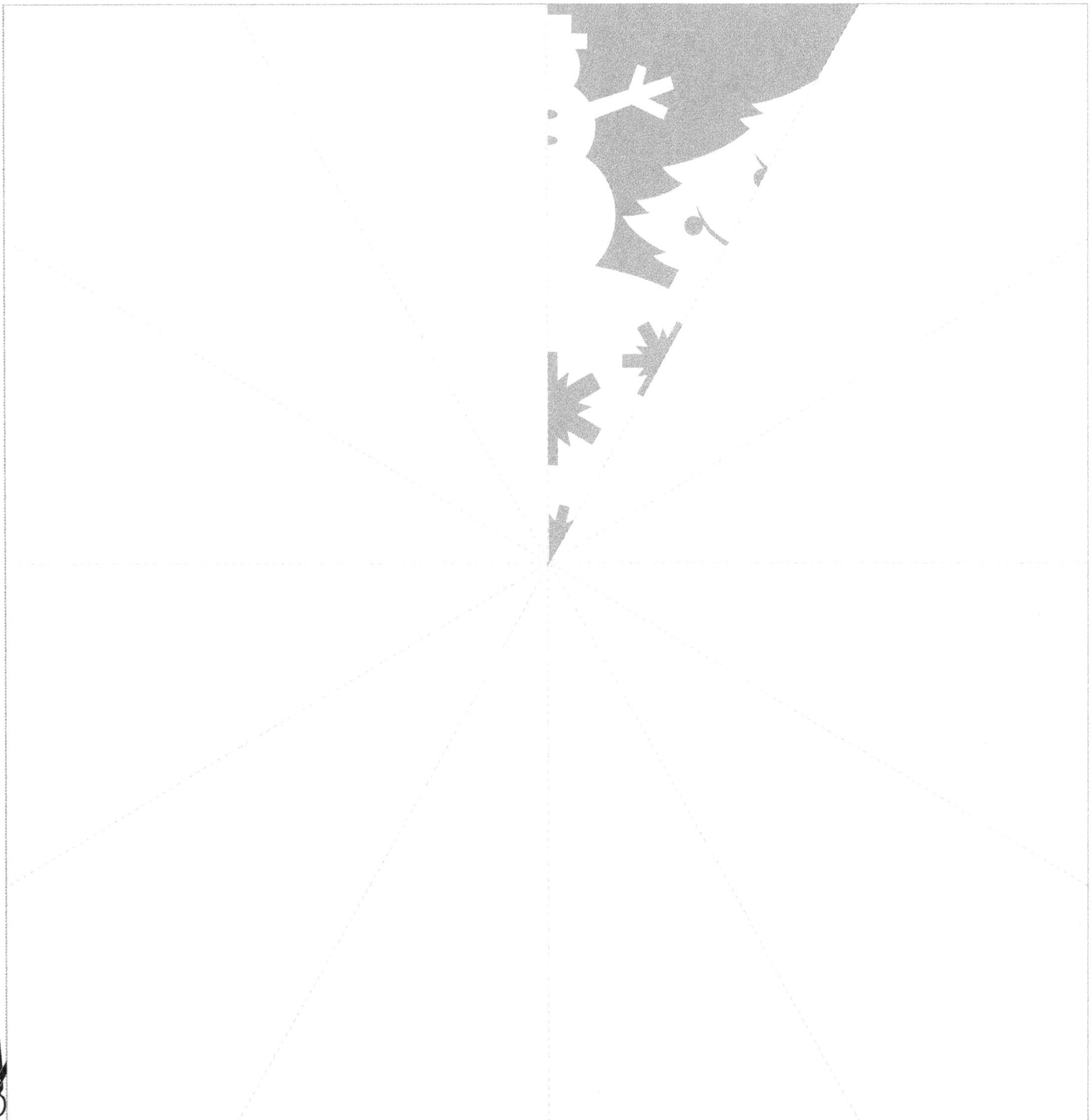

Snowmen
6 Pointed, Getting Harder

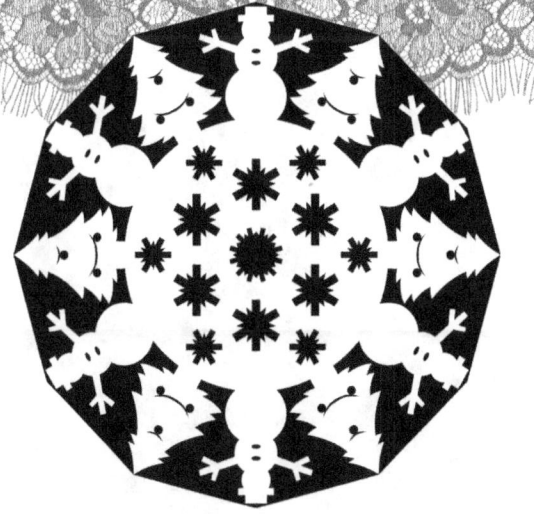

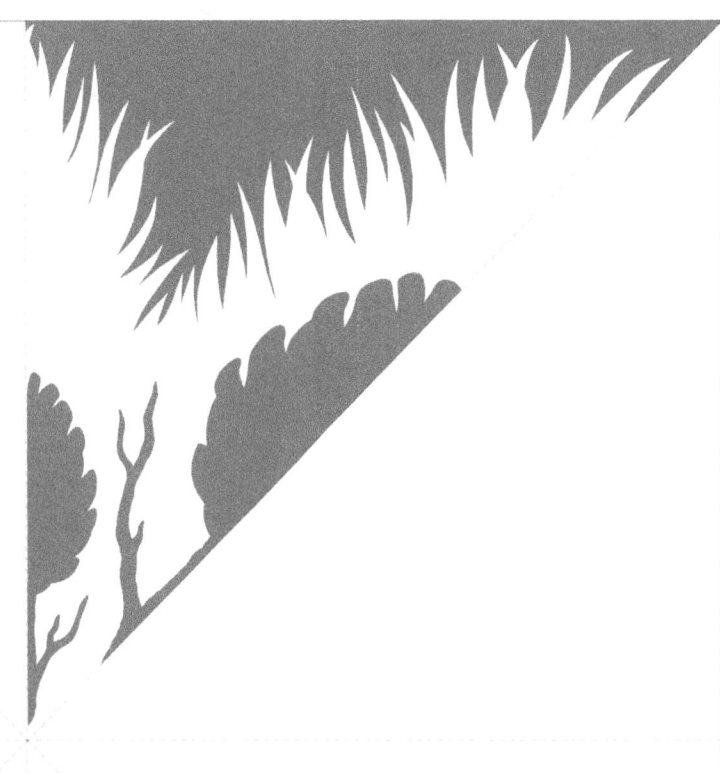

Pinebough
4 Pointed, Getting Harder

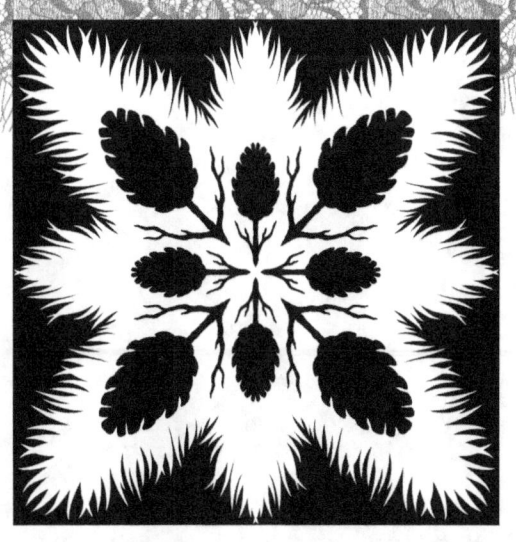

Snowglobe
6 Pointed, Getting Harder

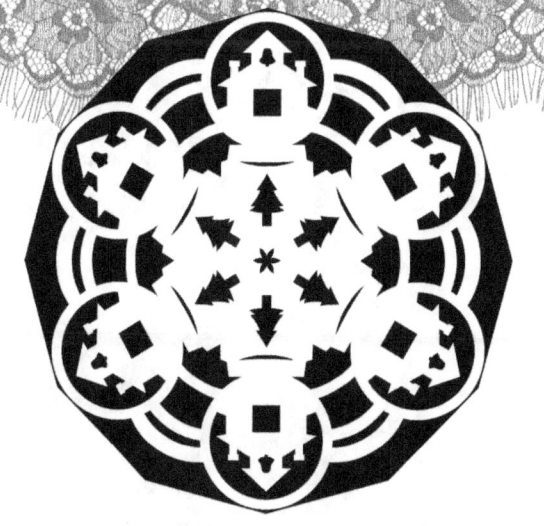

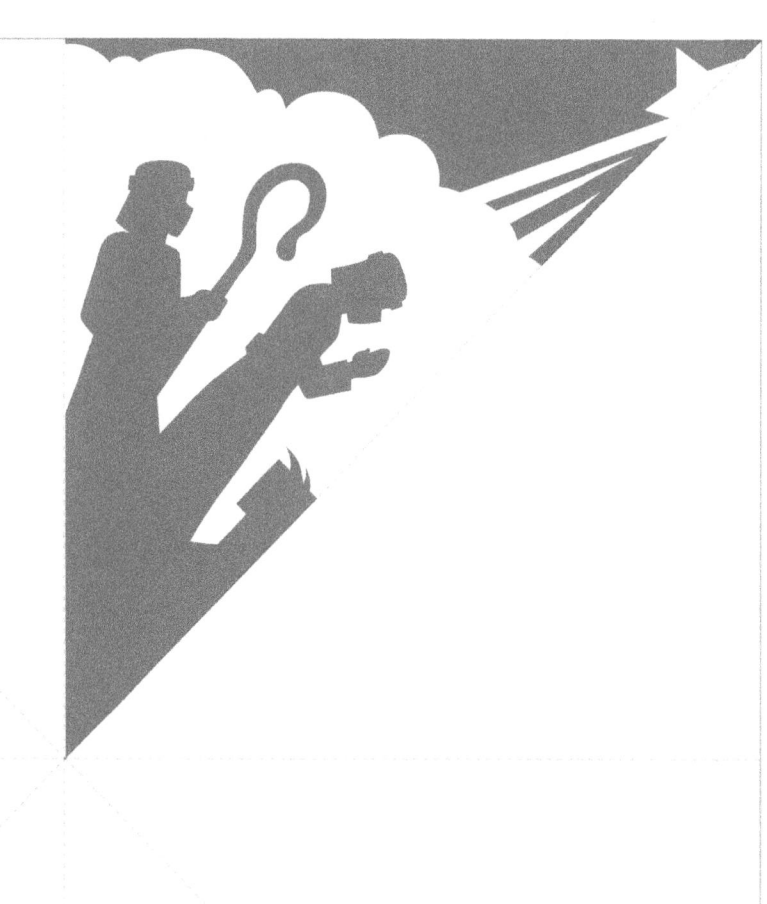

Shepherds
4 Pointed, Very Hard

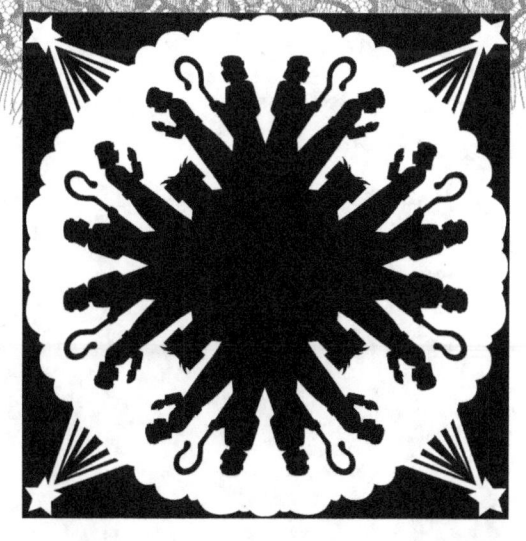

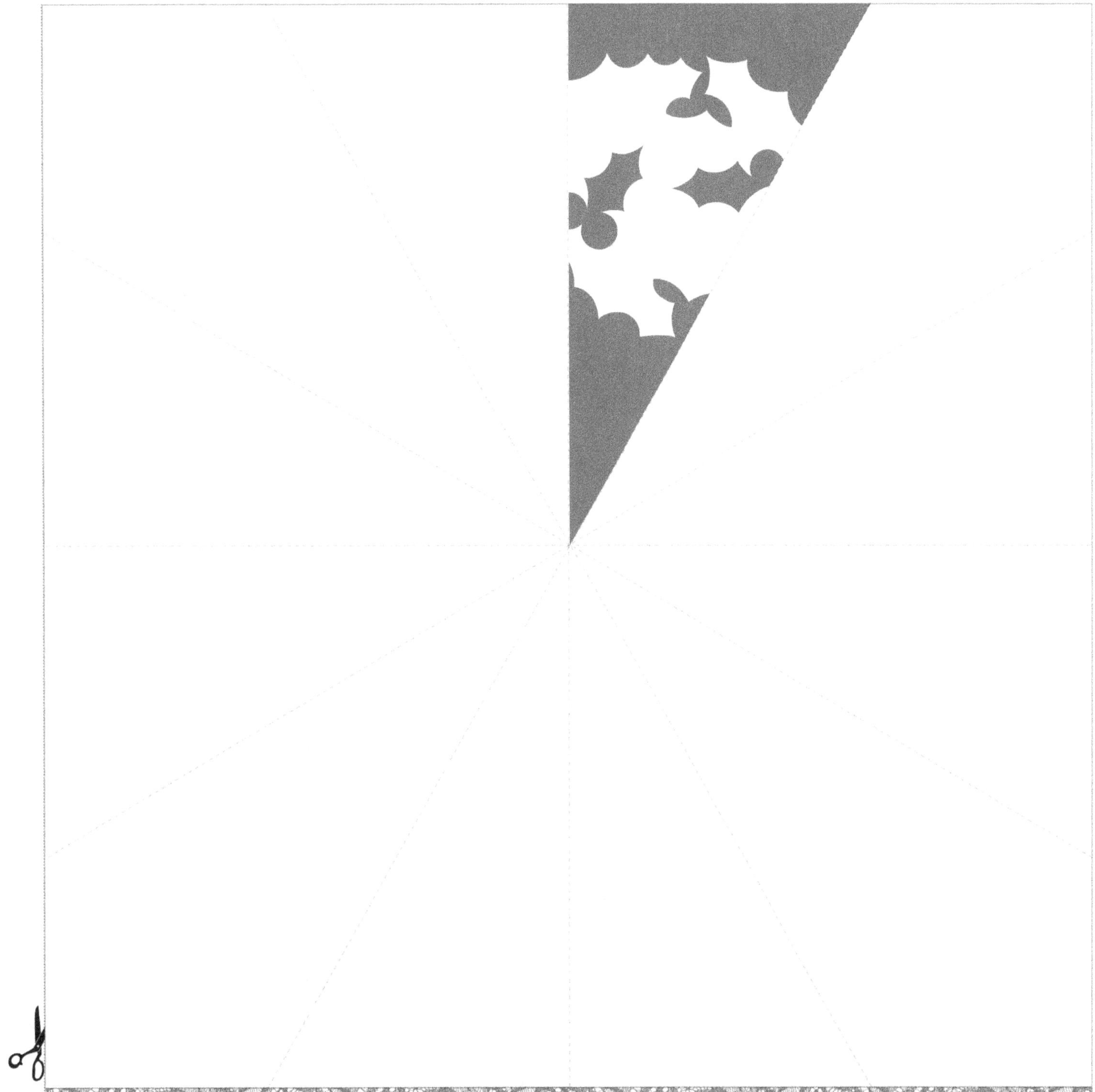

Holly Wreath

6 Pointed, Very Hard

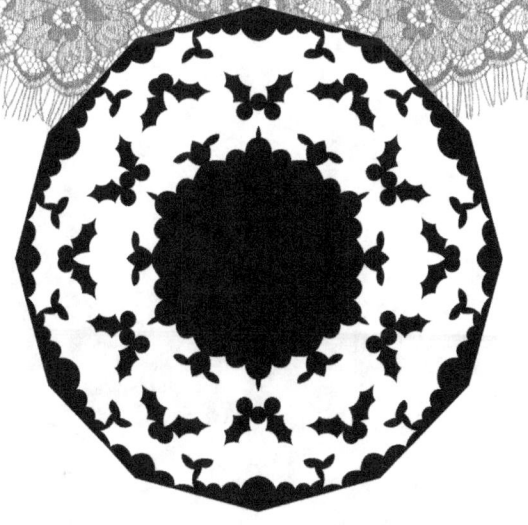

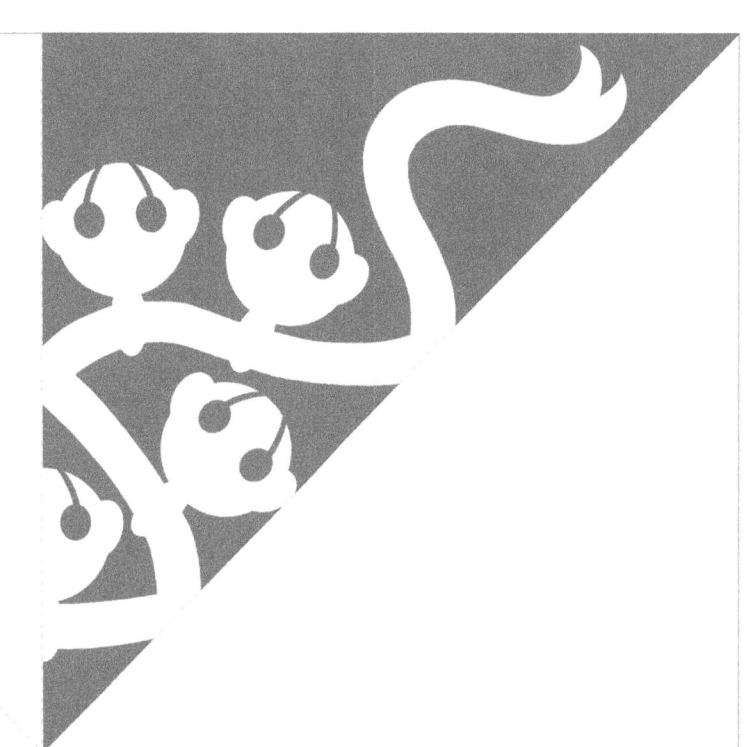

Jingle Bells
4 Pointed, Very Hard

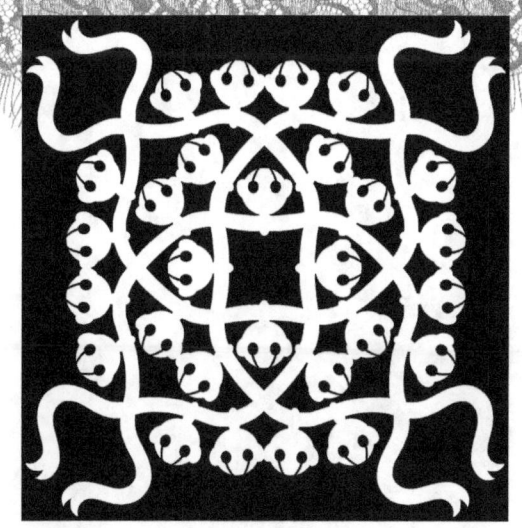

Reindeer
6 Pointed, Holy Smokes!

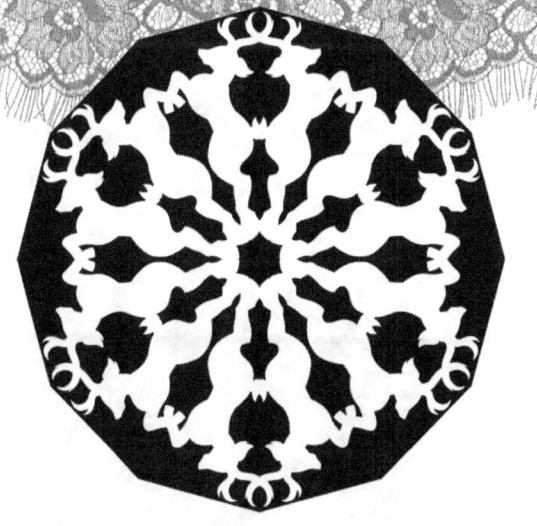

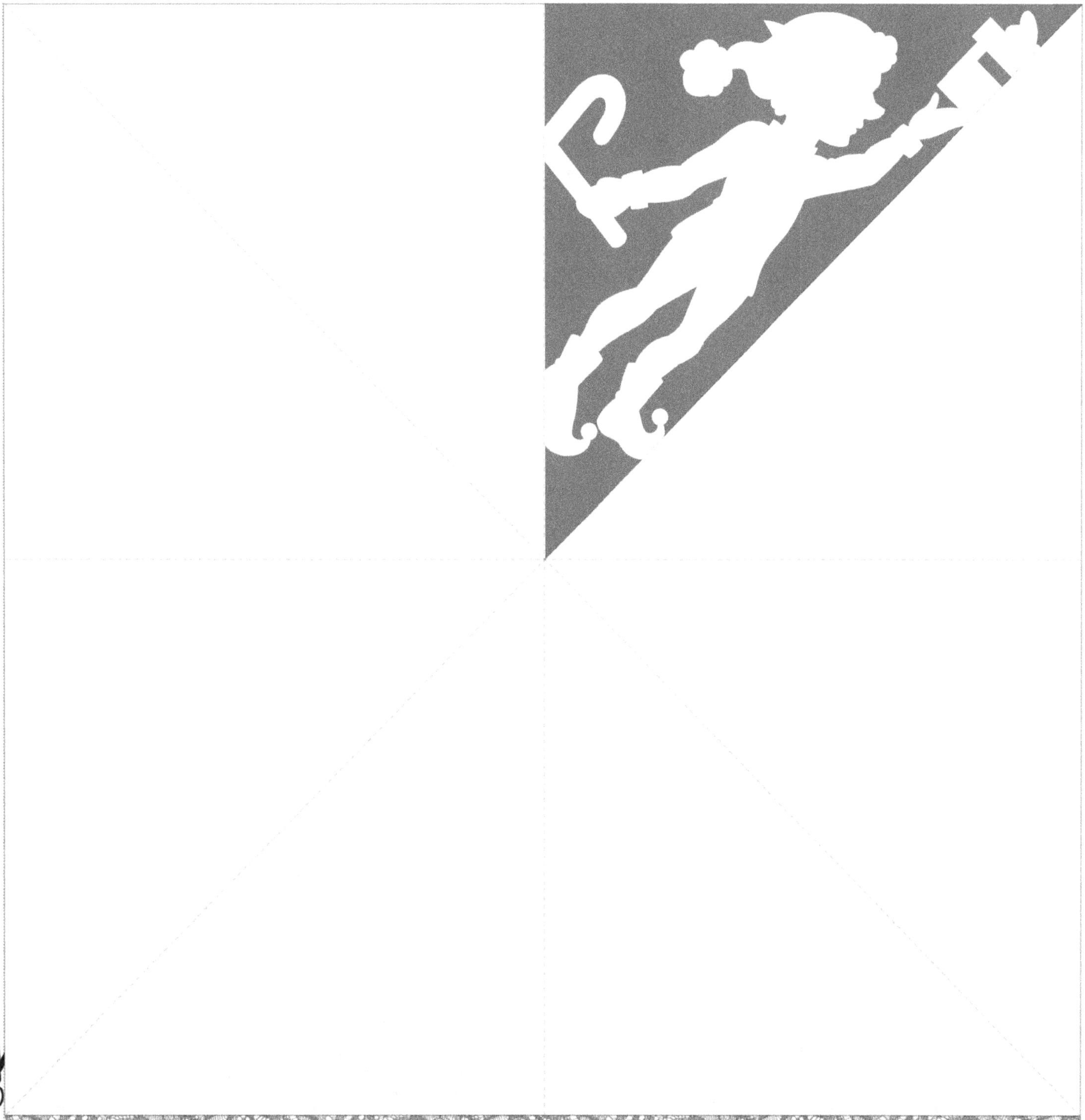

Elves
4 Pointed, Holy Smokes!

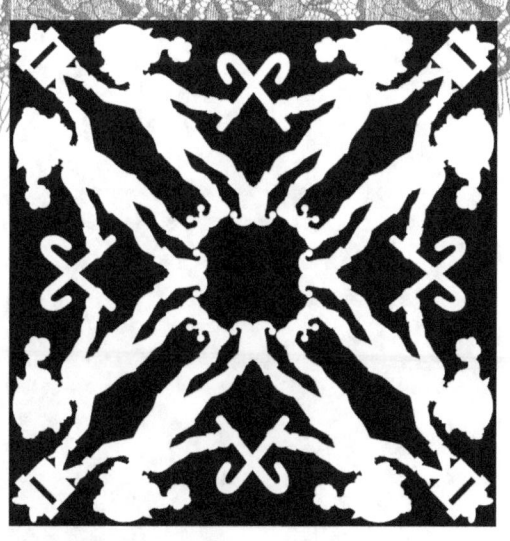

21

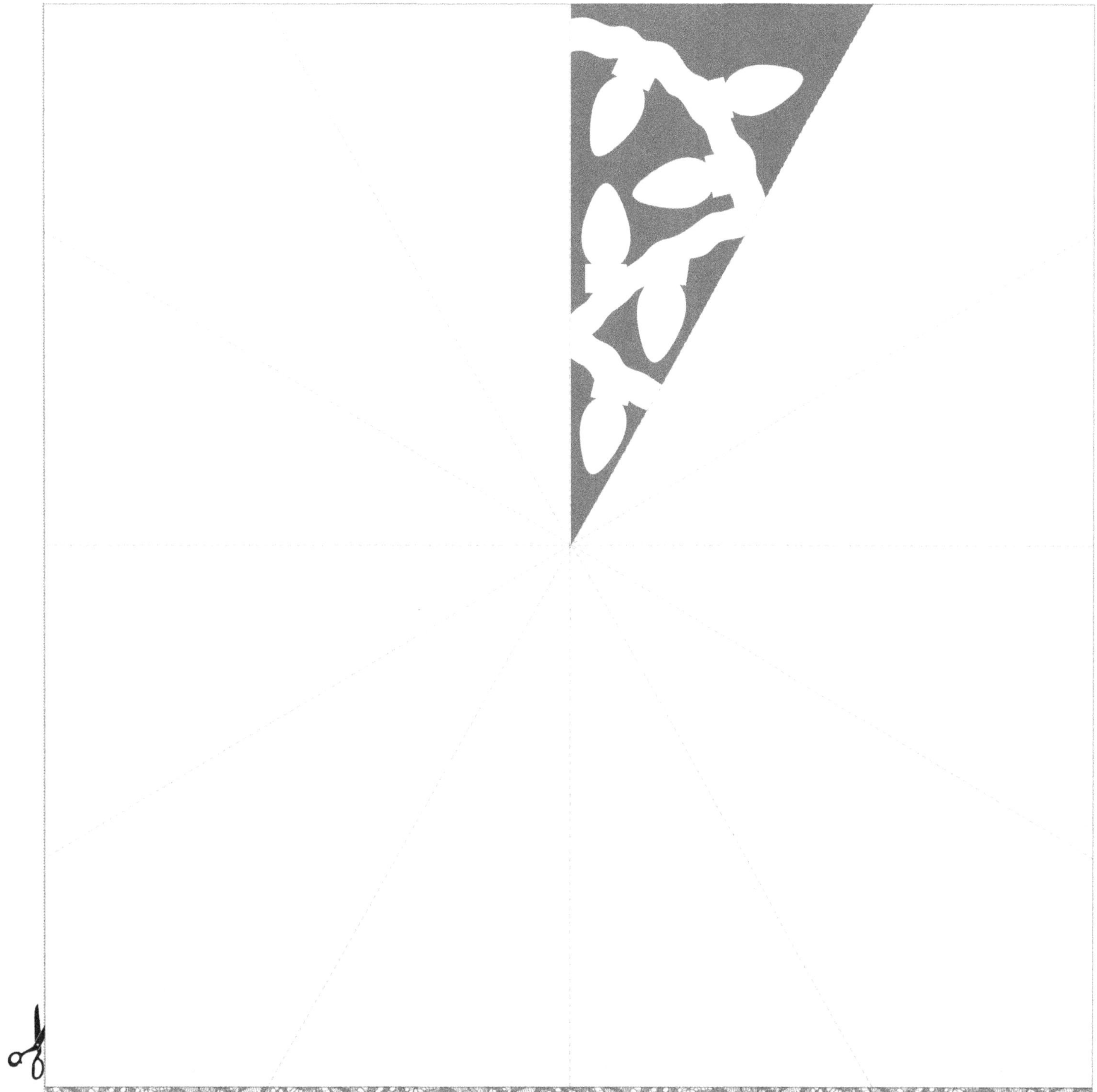

Light Tangle
6 Pointed, Holy Smokes!

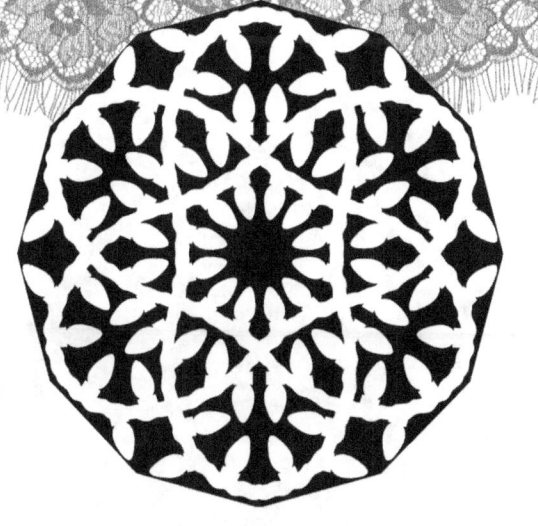

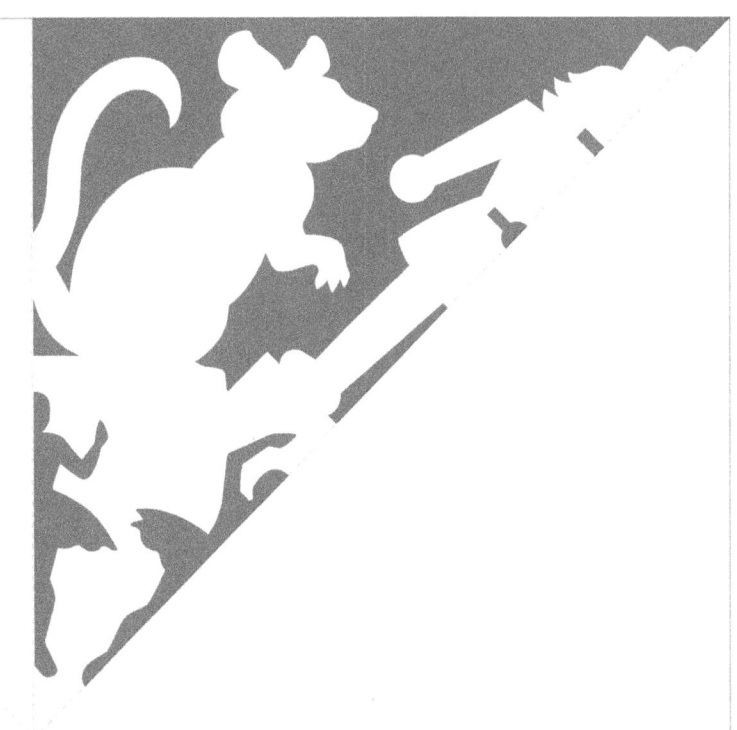

Nutcracker Suite

4 Pointed, Holy Smokes!

Index

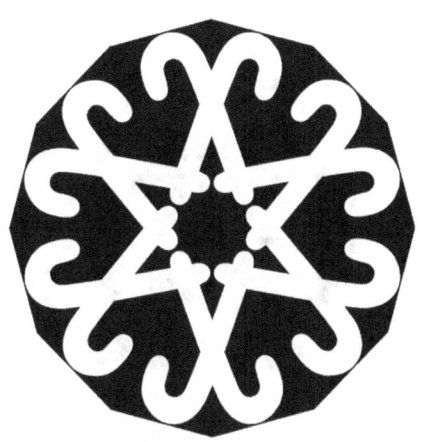
Candy Canes, pg 4

Poinsettia, pg 5

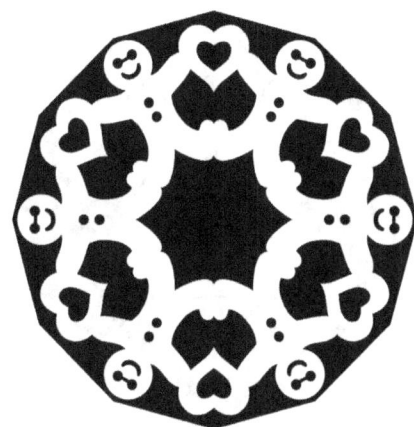
Gingerbread Man, pg 6

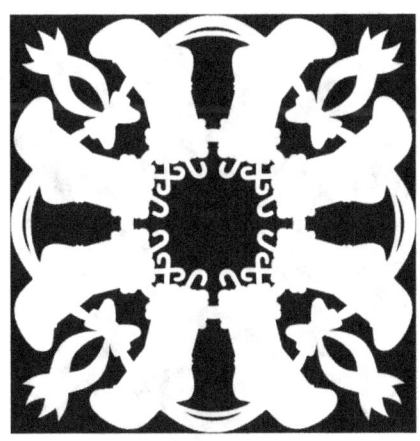
Stockings, pg 7

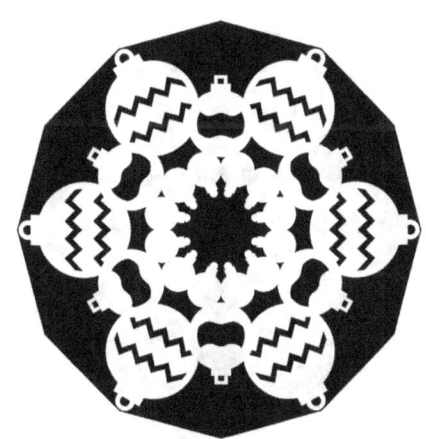
Ornaments, pg 8

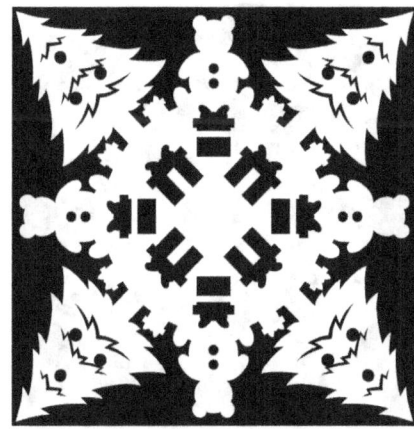
Presents under the Tree, pg 9

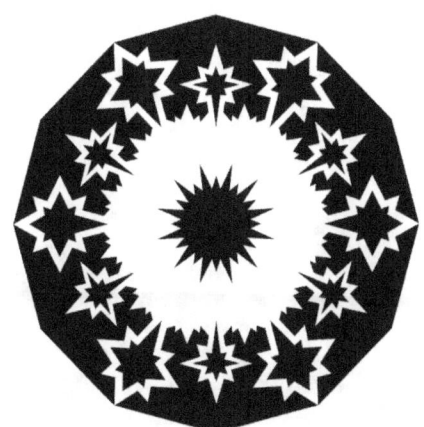
Star of Bethlehem, pg 10

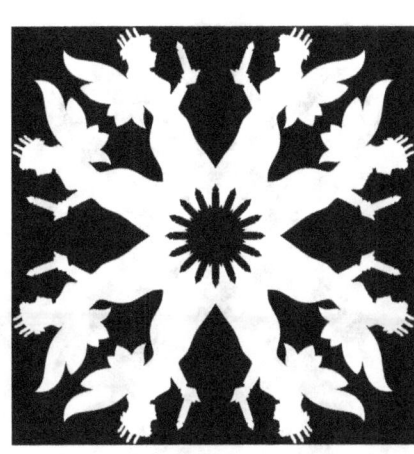
Saint Lucia, pg 11

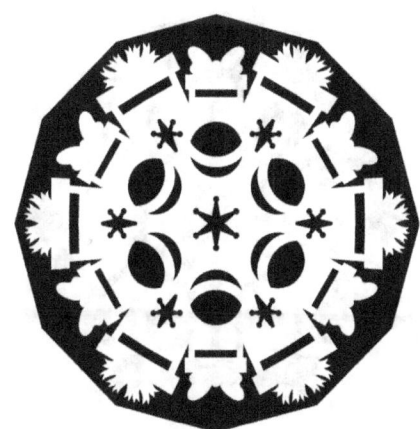
Jacks, pg 12

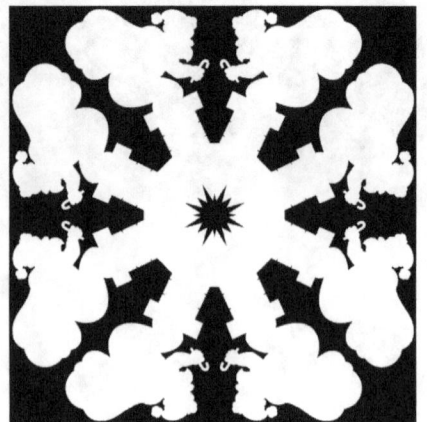
Santa, pg 13

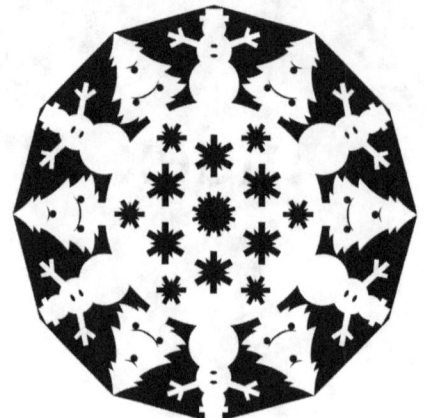
Snowmen, pg 14

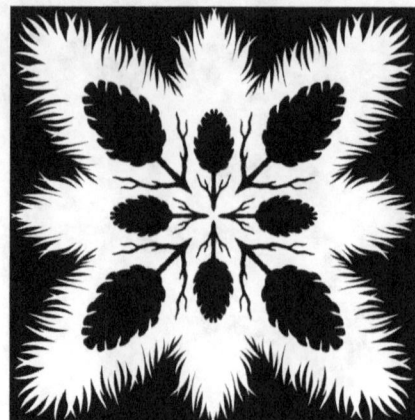
Pinebough, pg 15

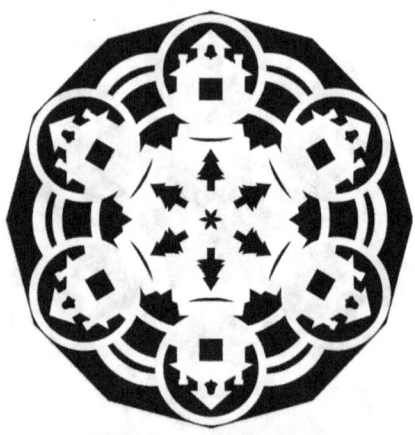
Snowglobe, pg 16

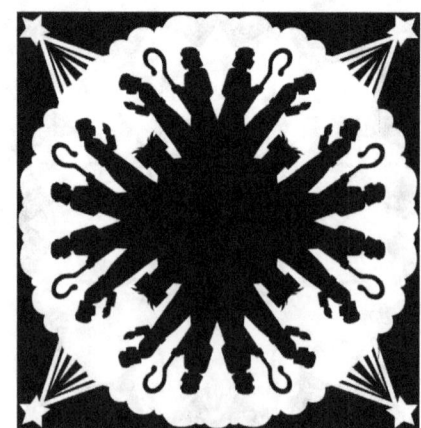
Shepherds, pg 17

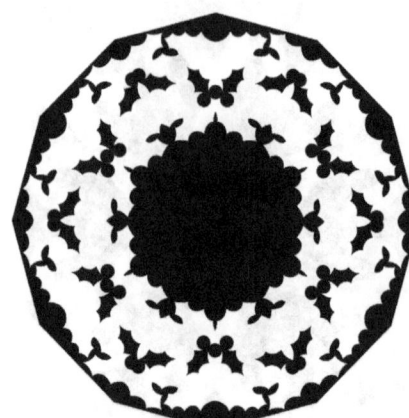
Holly Wreath, pg 18

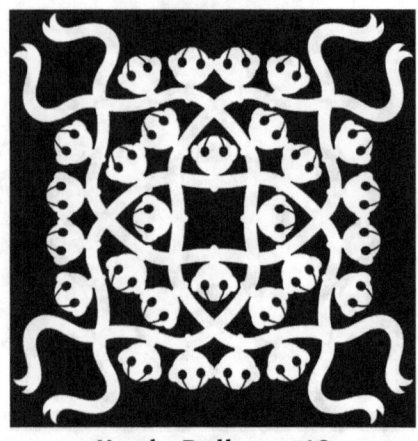
Jingle Bells, pg 19

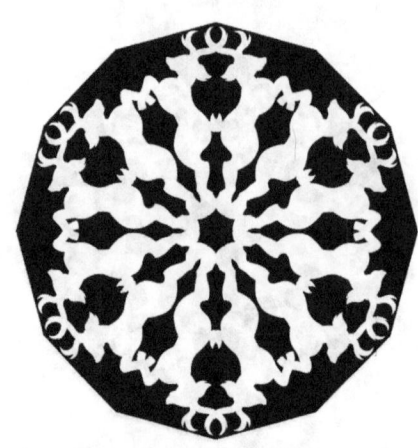
Reindeer, pg 20

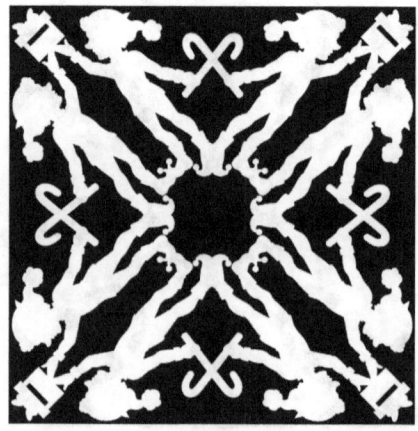
Elves, pg 21

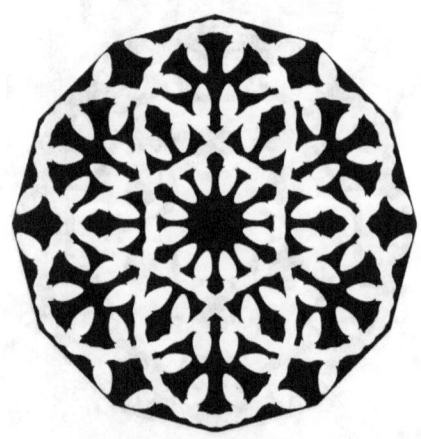
Light Tangle, pg 22

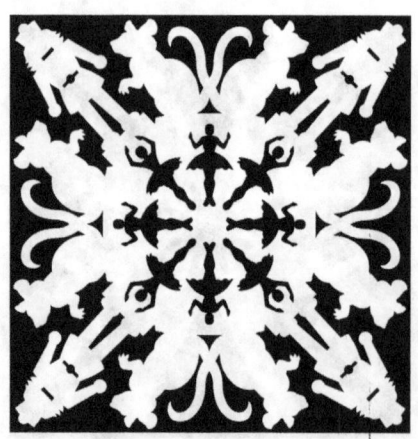
Nutcracker Suite, pg 23

www.ingramcontent.com/pod-product-compliance
Lightning Source LLC
Chambersburg PA
CBHW080444220526
45465CB00007B/2759